Republican Fathers

Poems by
Ralph James Savarese

NINE MILE BOOKS

Publisher: Nine Mile Art Corp.
Editors: Bob Herz, Stephen Kuusisto, Andrea Scarpino
Assistant Editor: Diane Wiener
Cover Art: Photograph courtesy of the Library of Congress. "Easter
Monday Egg Roll," *Frank Leslie's Illustrated Newspaper*, 23 April 1887

Republican Fathers

The publishers gratefully acknowledge support of the New York State
Council on the Arts with the support of Governor Andrew M. Cuomo
and the New York State Legislature. We also acknowledge support of the
County of Onondaga and CNY Arts through the Tier Three Project
Support Grant Program. We have also received significant support from
the Central New York Community Foundation. This publication would
not have been possible without their generous support. We are grateful to
them all.

ISBN-13: 978-1-7326600-9-0

ACKNOWLEDGEMENTS

I gratefully acknowledge the editors of the following journals in which some of these poems, some in earlier versions, first appeared: *American Poetry Review, Bridge Eight, Cream City Review, The Haven, Love's Executive Order, Nine Mile Magazine, Psaltery and Lyre, Rattle, Seneca Review,* and *Stone Canoe.*

For their encouragement and/or helpful comments, I wish to thank Dean Bakopoulos, Nancy Barber, Pilar Martinez Benedi, David Blake, John Lee Clark, Eileen Chow, Page Coulter, Marty Dobrow, Fran Dorf, David Dunbar, Susannah Goodman, Elizabeth Graver, Bob Herz, Emily Hipchen, Michael Hofmann, Deborah Jenson, Emery Jenson, Steve Kuusisto, Dawn-Joy Leong, Chris Martin, Johanna Meehan, Mark Montgomery, Jack Carlos Mindich, Jeremy Mindich, Joe Neisser, Suzanne Paola, Jeff Porter, Tinker Powell, F.D. Reeve, Andres Rojas, Lisa Ruddick, D.J. Savarese, Emily Savarese, Peter Sokol, Olga Solomon, Nick Sousanis, Nathan Spoon, Maura Strassberg, David Weiss, Judith Weld, and Tilly Woodward.

CONTENTS

For Jeremy Mindich
and
John T. Paoletti

*"Bring along a new novel with you some time, will you, only
please not one of those modern ones."*

"What do you mean, grand-maman?"

*"I mean the kind in which the hero strangles his parents or
someone drowns in a river. I have a terrible fear of drowned
people."*

—Alexander Pushkin, "The Queen of Spades"

PREFACE

When James Baker, Chief of Staff under Ronald Reagan and Secretary of State under George Herbert Walker Bush, was asked what he had learned about his time in Washington, he replied, "Power is fleeting." Then, as if delivering a homily at church, he related this anecdote. Once, approaching the White House gates in a limousine, he noticed a man walking on Pennsylvania Avenue. The man, he soon realized, had been Secretary of State in a previous administration. "There he was alone," Baker said. "No reporters, no security, no adoring public, no trappings of power. Just one solitary man alone with his thoughts."

The former secretary was right, if a bit narrow in his judgment: *everything* is fleeting. Readers under 40 may fail to recognize the names in this book: John Ehrlichman, Elliot Richardson, Frank Carlucci, William Safire, Alexander Haig—all of them players in the Republican Party during the 70s, 80s, and early 90s, and all of them quite rich. These men now walk the avenues of history. As with shades in the underworld, it's hard to make out their faces. Some, like Baker himself, continue to invest in oxygen.

To me, they tumble in the falls behind my house—the one I lived in as a teen in McLean, Virginia; the one that overlooked the River of Swans, as the Patawomeck called the great god spilling into Washington. Memory, like a baby, spits up on my shoulder, and out pops a once famous Republican. (There is no bib.) My connection to these men exceeds mere proximity, though I lived next door to two of them. Their children were my friends. Corruption was a family plot in whose pool we swam. Greed tucked us in at night—with or without love.

In my case, the political was not so much personal as pugilistic. Even a birthday card wore boxing gloves. Because my father was both a rich Republican and a violent narcissist, a link formed in my mind between party affiliation and parental performance. At school and at church, that link was ratified. My history teacher spoke of "Republican Fathers," and I promptly imagined Richard Nixon beating his children. (Rumors persist that he beat his wife, Pat.) With the rise of evangelical Christianity, God had become a Republican, and he, too, was a dad—an absent, nasty one who denounced gays and lesbians and, of course, women who had abortions.

The link was faulty, I know. It was based on an improper understanding of the adjective "republican" and a wild literalization of the noun "father." To me, the latter could never be just a metaphor—a way to give flesh to abstraction. (I had all the flesh I needed, and it hurt!) To say that Republicans make terrible papas is like eating ice cream in the rain and then forever connecting the two. And yet, where I lived as a teen, it seemed to rain all of the time.

In this volume, the error has grown up. It now works as a conceit—a kind of fireman or first responder to the scene.

I

A severe moralist would consider my frankness improper, but in the first place I can't conceal it, and then, as you know, I have always had my own particular principles about relations between father and son.

—Ivan Turgenev, *Fathers and Sons*

FACE TIME WITH THE PRESIDENT

1. Kitchen Cabinet

For years, I served in my father's administration,
begrudgingly, dutifully. In a minor cabinet post,
to be sure: Secretary of the Interior,
guardian of wild rumination, defender
of endangered feeling.... I'd been duped
by my President's smile, lured

from the comfortable sinecure, the truly private
sector, of baby food and diapers
by the soft rhetoric of devotion
and, I'm embarrassed to admit, the simple promise
of attention. Yet my President was rarely
around and almost never available.

For one thing, he had another job as a balding bigwig
in a large ANTI-TRUST law firm. (Why the voters
never penalized his lack of commitment
remains a mystery. I certainly wondered
if he really wanted to be President.)
A litigator who not only courted but also stalked

publicity and who became his firmament's
managing partner, he resembled nothing
so much as a gleaming, dictatorial cliché.
Like an action figure from Hasbro, Lawyer-man
came complete with Porsche, country-club
membership, and a spectacular palace

high above the Potomac (heart not
included). By age seven, my official portfolio
was sulking. At cabinet meetings,
I'd be dismissed as irrational, unmeasured,
and, the one I like best, insufficiently loyal.
"Why can't you get with the program?"

my President would shout. "Why can't you
be like the others—sufficiently fawning?" Sometimes,
when a discussion grew heated, my President
would accost me, hurling my head against a wall
like some official in Iraq whom Saddam
himself had decided personally to reprimand

(the Supreme Commander wanting to be sure
everyone understood his supreme dissatisfaction).
More often than not, I'd have just come
to the defense of the First-of-Many-Ladies,
who despised her husband. After such a meeting,
I'd pick myself up with as much dignity

as a humiliated cabinet member could muster
and wander out to the deck behind our palace.
There, in the ordinary spectacle of the falls,
I'd find a form of solace. The river hardly ever
seemed ruffled: it just kept falling, just kept babbling
its subtle protest. (Safely in high school,

I'd come to think of the river as an exasperated
Gandhi, practicing its civil disobedience,
offering up its murmurous indictment,
and occasionally swallowing a swimmer or seven.)
To the right, at a distance, lived Elliot Richardson,
Nixon's Attorney General; to the left,

Francis Carlucci, Reagan's National Security Advisor.
The neighborhood, if you could call it that,
was filled with the rich and sourful.
I remember seeing Mr. Richardson regularly
on his deck a year or so after he'd resigned.
He seemed to share my habit of investigating

the falls. Once, he even waved to me, as if
understanding my plight. "Mr. Richardson,"
I called out to him, "Mr. Richardson,"
but not before he had turned to go inside.
Mostly, we embattled politicos kept
to ourselves. Years later, when the Gipper

came to Mr. Carlucci's house for dinner, the river
filled with Secret Service agents: some
were in pontoon boats, some were actually
in the heckling water itself. We'd been instructed
to remain indoors that evening, and, hence,
from a window with the lights off,

I watched the convoluted operation: suited secrecy
like a colonizing mist. "They're here to protect
me," my President announced, and, for a moment,
it seemed as if there had been some sort
of extraordinary mix-up, as if—could it be?—
the Advance Team had gotten not only the wrong address

but also the wrong man. After all, my President
was President! And yet, as much as my President
seemed to require protection, he also seemed,
through some feat of personal psychology,
to have rendered such protection obsolete. Less
a human flack-jacket than a holograph or phantom,

he just couldn't be gotten to. Still, I responded,
"Protect you from what? Your family?" By
this point, about halfway through my President's
fourth term, I'd begun to fight back at cabinet meetings,
to the horror of the First-of-Many-Ladies,
who plaintively reminded me, again and again,

that I served at the pleasure of the President.
Yet even as I loathed my President, I stupidly
searched for him, fancying myself the Secretary
of *His* Interior: a vast space, from what I imagined,
given over to developers of a distinctly egotistical
and commercial persuasion. Rather, he was like

Alaska at the turn-of-the-century—in need
of surveying. Except none of the surveyors
had ever made it back: all of them lost in the dark
and cold, all of them dead from hypothermia.
Their tiny, frozen tents entombed by snow. When
I say that I wouldn't have wanted even a distant

Ambassadorship—something on the Island
of Oedipal Relief or in the Republic of Reciprocal
Devotion—you shouldn't believe me. For there
I was, having never been confirmed, having never
even really been appointed, clamoring like all
of the other sycophants for face time with the President.

2. Sacred Constitution

Not once but twice I dreamt that my siblings and I
were my President's teeth, assembled for a dreaded
policy meeting (read: tribute to the King).

A darker, danker, more crowded and malodorous
room you cannot imagine! My President
had, by this point, let his pearly White House go.

Periodontitis had marched into the capital
like the British in 1812. At first we molars
resembled something of a compost heap and, then,
a sewage drain. You couldn't be anywhere
near us so badly did we stink. A man of his
resources, his unwavering self-regard, refusing

to engage a dentist? Who more needed a chaplain
to the lateral and central incisors, a father confessor
to the delicate, vascular pulp—the soul!—
that lay inside? His refusal perplexed me. After all,
my President had built himself a gym, hired
a personal trainer, attended to his pecs, his abs,

his quads, his calves—those lovely grounds around
the People's House. Why not his teeth? (The members
of my President's firmament were similarly perplexed.
Although worried about their corporate face,
they felt too embarrassed to say anything. Once,
at a party, a junior partner asked me if my President

had ever seen a dentist.) His refusal surely
had to do with his pathological penchant
for control. No celestial ruler could lie
prostrate in a chair, someone else's hands inside
his policy meeting. Nor could he tolerate
a sanctimonious sermon on neglect—

having to play the part of the toothy schoolboy
who hadn't studied for his test. Picture Everyking

before his daily grave, the morning mirror,
willfully missing the hissing message of decay.
Was there no limit to what my President
could overlook? In the dream, he's eating

sour balls and discoursing on himself. The sugar's
killing us—such sickly sweet self-adulation!
I want to stage a coup. I want to be his tongue,
the Chief of Staff! Make him formulate some other
words: a simple sentiment I've never heard;
make him renounce his fundamental loyalty,

his sacred constitution, like those televised P.O.W.s
in Vietnam. And yet surely, like them, he'd
be able to signal with his eyelids that he wasn't
being genuine: "I do not love them; I love myself.
I do not love them; I love myself," batted
meticulously in Morse Code. Over the years,

we nearly all were fired or resigned. I went out
like Mr. Richardson in a phase of glory: a kind
of Saturday Night Massacre—a principled extraction
against my President's foul deceitfulness. (He'd tried
to screw the First-of-Many-Ladies in a divorce
settlement.) Only my shameless sister remained,

like Kissinger with Nixon, waiting for that final
helicopter: death's noisy but ever so agile touchdown.
My President's career long over; his body gone
to the dogs (his money, though, still working out
furiously on a treadmill at the bank). She was, I now
think, that yellowed but stubborn front tooth

in the rotten oval office of his mouth.

PAPER BOY

Poor Bob Ehrlichman,
our paperboy when I was ten.
Spawn of Tricky Dick's right hand man—

or one of two such fists,
the other being H.R. Haldeman.
Dual Chiefs of Wrath, they built

a Berlin wall around the President.
(Insiders joked about a single *Herdleman*.)
A big kid, bigger than his fifteen years

and not the least reliable, Bob hurled
the morning's headlines at our house:
History's sodden missive,

History's poorly aimed, if not unguided,
surface-to-air missile. His father
thought he needed extra tutoring

in the bootstrap philosophy of Horatio Alger.
Sometimes, Bob would hurl the paper
at our bushes or cars;

sometimes, not at all.
Did he believe himself immune
to his missiles' impact? Believe himself

a kind of junior punisher—
not Nixon's but the neighborhood's
"son of a bitch"? Or was he angry

with his dad, everywhere
in the papers yet never around?
(Everywhere in the papers

and causing him trouble at school:
the pitiful glances, the whispering,
"I hear his Dad's going to jail.")

All fall, stories of the cover-up
had proliferated like guinea pigs
in a child's bedroom.

A lesson, I imagine, in lower math:
compounding charges and deception,
the political having become

a bit too personal, a bit
too *sexual*, what with our carrier's
obvious hormonal rebellion.

(When your father's a Republican
there are simply too many reasons
to want to sleep with your mother.)

Who knows what Bob thought?
His diligence when delivering word
of his begetter's indictment

was certainly uncharacteristic. It seemed
pointed—one might even say *pregnant*
were it not for the baggie

in which the paper was wrapped.
That morning he placed it
ever so gently into our primping portico.

PAPER MAN

Any news from the underworld, Bob?
On a whim, I Googled your name
this morning and discovered
that you had died.

Death is digital now. We embalm everything,
even the paper. Your smile stared
back up at me, as at
a wake.

The coffin, that space on my computer
screen, had no sides or bottom.
It lay like an infant on my lap.
It gave off heat....

You were only 55, had been married
twice, were a doting father—if
the obit can be believed.
You know journalists,

Bob, they often get the story wrong.
Your father detested them.
What you delivered as
a teen was lies,

all lies and, anyway, the product of leaks.
In his role as chief White House
plumber, he should have
followed Ahab,

that other Nixon, who had the sense
to say, "Let it leak. I'm all aleak

myself. Aye! Leaks
in leaks!"

Withdrawing his appeal, your father reported
early to prison in New Mexico, said
he couldn't abide the wait,
the uncertainty.

The idea of prison had blossomed in his
mind like the *Amorphophallus
titanum*, whose stink
attracts

a particular kind of pollinator: insects that
dump their eggs in elapsed organisms
or feast on such a delicacy.
Its stink is greatest

at midnight. The spadix of flowers
can rise, like Tricky Dick himself,
almost ten feet. What
penal tumescence!

He had to get it over with. Yet, prison,
your father soon realized, the kind
that he had been sent to—
a broom and glove

factory with two tennis courts—was
no worse than being in the army.
Unlike the Iron Chancellor,
who tested sewage

at a treatment facility, he waited until
he got out to deal in waste,

nuclear waste. I think
I understand

what your father was feeling. Every so
often, I feel that way about
the prison hereafter.
"Let's get it over

with," I say. "Let's do my timelessness
now." Maybe there's even a tennis
court.... In this life's howling
gale, change,

I suppose, is possible. Your father became
a hippie of sorts, accepted a small
portion of responsibility,
moved on

to other women, another child. Maybe
the two of you got along just fine.
But did you ever really forgive
his War on Drugs,

which was designed, he admitted, to create
a problem that Nixon could solve and
then, by solving, crush the Left?
Black people and heroin:

a bad, *advertising bundle*, yet ever so
effective at the polls. Hey, Mr. *Paper
Boy* (thanks to Google, I learned
some slang this morning),

let's go *chase the tiger*. This *jolly pop* needs
some *courage pills*, some *reindeer dust*,

some *white china*…. Here's what
I remember

of the summer your father was indicted.
You wrecked my soap-box derby
racer, smashed it to bits and
did so on purpose.

Though you were too big for it, I let you
have a ride. I wanted you to like me,
sensed we had something in
common. At the end

of our steep driveway, you turned the steering
mechanism sharply and rolled. I watched
the wheels come off, the base break
in two. I ran down

after you, and you were laughing, laughing
uproariously, like a man at the gallows
who seeks to preserve his honor.
(We lived, back then, on

Neuse Way.) Call it divided government:
your knees and elbows wept—you had
cuts everywhere. The obit didn't
mention how you had died.

SINKERS

A homophone for cola
(Colonel Pemberton's variety)

or an 80s recreational drug,
his name meant nothing to me

at the time, though the lanky,
East European blonde

by his side—I want to say,
in his lap—certainly drew

my attention.
She was an artist of sorts,

working in various media
and states of undress.

With her Isabey Kolinsky
watercolor breasts,

she painted *THE BORED*
OF TRUSTEES

AT THEIR AUTUMNAL PALACE
(which had once been attacked

by the Pocumtuc tribe
and then, centuries later,

became the Headmaster's House).
The school was a paean

to noble testosterone.
Blue-blooded, blue balled,

the boys would monetize
tomorrow—

even their sperm drove Maseratis.
On campus, spring was brought

to you by Citi Bank or Chase:
bikini-waxed shrubs, green-suited

trees standing tall and true....
And everywhere a shrine

with some industrialist's
name on it. *You're only*

as happy as your last erection.
At the dinner, I sat across

from the artist
and her Medici patron

who sensed my discomfort,
no doubt chalking it up

to my not having come
from money.

Not having cum from money?
Trust me, I came—

again and again.
My parents were a bank

from which I repeatedly
withdrew....

Dorm master, teacher and coach,
I was to exteriorize

institutional devotion
as the development pickpockets

took to the sky and like locusts
swarmed the ears

of these well-endowed men.
Oh, the dulcet tones of flattery—

the very air seemed carbonated.
The soon-to-be life-time

trustee spoke of skiing
in the Alps;

I watched a pupil navigate
the white slope of his eye—

fresh snow had fallen.
For the rich, vision

is a peak from which to scoff
at the laboring world.

The next day,
I caught my new friends

making art in the woods.
He was like a dog on top of her

as she leaned against a tree.
They were supposed to be

watching the sports teams
on the lower fields—

we were all
athletic supporters,

throwing money into cups.
I had slipped away to pee

and spotted the pair
not fifty feet from the river

where *A Better Chance*
boy from Harlem

had drowned the year before
while swimming

with his peers.
Given a blazer and two pairs

of pants, he had been told
to fit in.

Be true to your heritage—
that heritage hadn't taught him

how to swim.
"There are sinkers and there

are risers. The boy
was a sinker,"

a colleague had said.
I can still hear his sister's sobs.

The school paid for both
the funeral and death—

got quite a deal, I would say.
A few years after I quit,

I saw my favorite libertine on TV.
There had been an accident

at LAX, with one plane landing
on top of another.

A jet had fucked its smaller,
turboprop counterpart,

killing everyone on board—
even some on the bigger plane died.

The trustee had had to fight
his way out, pushing

and shoving—
there was soot on his forehead.

Oh, the unregulated markets
of survival!

The man was definitely
a riser.

When the black boy's peers
were interviewed,

one said, "No one noticed
that he was gone."

ASK, TELL

We were sixth-graders at middle-school camp,
conscripts in an old regime of the masculine,

privates third-class,
dreading the common shower,

the inevitable comparisons—
my own genital region like an unplanted field

far from a forest.
We didn't much care for our unit,

especially the bigger boys, lords of the rise
they got out of you,

bullies snapping their towels,
giving someone a wedgie.

Two hours into the trip and you were miserable:
a sullen lump on the rope swing.

The second night, after the ghost stories
and guitar, after the game

of capture the flag,
after the Walton family imitations

("Night, John Boy. Night, Mary Ellen"),
you showed up at my bed—unannounced,

shivering, distraught.
"I'm cold," you whispered, tapping me

on the shoulder. "I'm cold."
And I, drowsy with sleep,

thinking you were my baby sister
scared of a thunderstorm,

or not thinking at all, told you
to crawl in.

**

And that's how, the next morning,
our gym teacher found us:

in the same zipped-up sleeping bag,
the same sweaty, blue cocoon of dreams.

Remember trying to scramble back to consciousness?
Suddenly, a voice loud enough to wake

the other boys:
"WHAT ARE YOU TWO DOING?"

Like a street urchin flushed from an underground city,
you maneuvered through winding

passageways and inky, muck-filled sewers
to locate a manhole.

Then lifting the cumbersome lid,
you rose into shame—I right behind you.

**

Say we were two boys together clinging
(that's how Whitman once put it),

two boys wrapped in goose-feather affection,
our skulls propped against one another

like pick-up sticks, sunlight
pouring into the musty cabin, splashing

on the walls—dawn once again at it
with her water cannon.

All that muscle-crowned gym teacher
could talk about was sex

and a word (sodomy) we didn't understand.
His fellow chaperone, the guidance counselor,

insisted on phoning our fathers.
"What they need is a good man-to-man."

Yours was hysterical—let us say,
representatively so.

Three tears for the moderate Republican
from Maine, that toupee-ed paradox!

He saw the future as a carpet at last unrolled,
a red one ruined by moths.

So much for ever being President....
Mine, the corporate lawyer,

made a motion
to hold me in contempt.

**

Must a boy swim upstream for miles and then
like a salmon agreeably die?

What has become of you,
my disconsolate bedmate?

Are you able to follow the federal guidelines
on loneliness,

that preposterous compromise?
You can *be* lonely,

but you can't tell anyone,
nor can anyone ask.

If I had to guess: you're probably married now
with children,

an amiable enough, country-club sort
of citizen, a lobbyist or defense contractor

preaching the gospel of national security
while taking advantage of pop's

incomparable connections.
(The old man like a base-runner

stranded at third,
having made it to congressman, then senator,

then the loyal opposition's
Pentagon head.)

**

Last night I saw your father,
the now former Secretary, on television.

He's been hired as a commentator
for the upcoming war.

"Soon, a squadron of bombers will swoop down
over Baghdad," he reported, "dropping

their loads, doing their dirty business
in the dark." Well,

he didn't say that exactly,
though his enthusiasm *was* nearly sexual.

America has begun its chant;
outside, even the cicadas are preparing

for combat, pounding their thoraxes.
In the first Gulf conflict,

pilots were given pornographic materials
as a motivational tool.

"Go out and give it to her," the men joked
as they climbed up to their cockpits.

Then lifting their cumbersome lids,
they rose into shame—

the entire country behind them.
So many miles, so much distance.

Look, the dead crawl into their body bags
alone. Remember playing

beneath the streets? Remember the warmth
of my breath on your shoulder?

There wasn't a girl between us
nor yet a dream of war.

THE JUSTICE AND MY FATHER

Long before he'd put his trust in antitrust litigation,
        defending high-profile companies from the charge
of monopolistic behavior, he'd dreamt of being on the court,
        and there he was, though not exactly in robes,
offering up his considered opinions: "Out!" "Out!" "Long!" "Long!"
        My father was playing Justice Stevens
in the annual Washington Golf and Country Club championships,
        the 1%er version of a constitutional battle.

The match seemed like something out of the WWF, complete
        with floodlights and a bellowing announcer:
"Weighing in at 200 pounds, the CORPORATE LITIGATOR
        with garish headband and flashy, graphite rackets;
weighing in at a meager 150, the FORD APPOINTEE
        with minimalist whites and old-fashioned *Jack Kramer*."
The racket, like the man, kept from warping by a nearly
        moral press. The audience for this contest:

straight from the crotch of Mammon. Junk-bond jocks
        and cum dividend panties, supply-side racketeers—
Reagan's Izod citizenry milling about the court, waiting for oral
        arguments to begin, as invariably they would begin
whenever my father fell behind. Great Ilie Nastase-like outbursts
        and finger gestures, the lunatic smashing of rackets.
It should have been a massacre yet wasn't, to everyone's surprise.
        At six-foot four, my father had planned

to serve the justice right off of the court, but the justice
        proved a formidable adversary,
finding a rebuttal to the slice out wide, the bomb down the T.

It was one of those matches in which a perfectly
respectable journeyman rises to persuasion, buoyed by the crowd,
        which, almost in spite of itself, applauds obstreperously.
A drop-shot here, an overhead there, a topspin lob well
        within the lines. They hardly knew

what they were clapping for, those tony Washingtonians.
        The more they clapped, the more perplexed
my father became, delivering his commentary on the match
        in noxious expletives and grunts, engaging
in highly audible deliberations: "How could anyone lose
        to this guy? Look at him: he's terrible!"
An originalist with respect to line calls, my father believed
        that the fuzzy, yellow globe was almost

always out—at least on his side of the court. ("Nowhere do
        the Founding Fathers speak of topspin.
Nowhere do they mention two-handed backhands.")
        And on the other? Well, just the opposite.
That side was a living rectangle, pliant, ready to accommodate
        any wayward or newfangled shot.
Before long, my father had stolen the second set. And still,
        the justice pressed on, surrendering points

he had won without a word—with only the rejoinder of his next
        miraculous shot: a backhand volley
angled into the corner, a forehand buggy-whip down the line,
        beyond the reach of the attacking originalist's outstretched arms.
Never had there been such an activist judge: shot-making
        without precedent. "Fuuuuuuuuuuck!" came the litigator's
steadfast reply. "Fuck your mealy-mouthed civility! Fuck
        your chicken-shit athleticism!"

"St. Imperturbable," I called him for the way he suffered
          my old man's antics, for the way he persevered.
Oh, how I wanted him to triumph—my stomach in knots as I pictured
          the ride home from the club. Rage at a hundred
miles an hour, the top down on car and cranium alike, my father
          complaining that *he*'d been hooked
by an unscrupulous opponent. What greater joy than the prospect
          of such misery in a Porsche? The car handling

so much better than he; a cop pulling us over.... Across the court
          sat the justice's daughter. Thoughts of treason
tugged at my groin. How many times had I seen her at the pool
          in the skimpiest of bikinis? Justitia herself lounging
by the ancient waters of fairness: bare-breasted, blindfolded, sword
          in one hand, scales in the other. How many times
had I played mixed doubles with her, always dreaming of the perfect
          match? 15-love, 30-love, 40-love and beyond,

the two of us married forever.... It was an eighth-grade relationship
          that never quite began. If only I had had the courage
to talk to her at the club, I could have married out of money and
          into noble principle, or so I thought back then.
(Ours, of course, was a strictly private judiciary, admitting neither
          Blacks nor Jews nor any ordinary capitalists.
Poor Clarence, no matter how white his shorts and shirt, could
          never have gotten in.) At five-all in the third,

the justice was clearly struggling. His strategy had been to remain
          on the court for as long as possible; he was in much
better shape than the lumbering litigator. Little did he know
          what a marathon it would be—the years piling up,
the administrations: Reagan, Reagan again, Bush, Clinton, Clinton
          again, Bush, Bush again. He wouldn't have

recognized himself at 80. Who plays tennis with a cane?
        "Hang on, Stevens, hang on!"

the crowd is crying, like some sort of chorus. They're doing
        the *Dikaiosune* wave, standing up for justice
with a capital—no, a lower-case—"j." Contradictions be praised!
        A Republican appointee who moved left?
A Republican appointee who *stayed put*, dug in, on a court, a landmass,
        lurching right. (How to spectate in the middle of an
earthquake? How to follow the bouncing ball?) When the dust
        settled, it settled for him, a less than super hero.

Justitia, what do you believe, now that you're a real-estate
        attorney and queen of commercial office space?
Have you forgiven your father his patrician airs and country club
        membership—Marx knows how many other
disappointments? Have you forgiven his tepid apology for capital?
        O checker of titles and escrow accounts,
private property's essential servant, have you forgiven yourself?
        Love wants no laws, no briefs, certainly no politics.

A few months back, I saw the two of you walking together:
        the lobbyists' K Street pyramids glimmered
in the sun—paean to transcendental money. How tenderly you
        took your father's arm and directed him through
traffic, the gridlocked cars impeding the crosswalk. It was as if
        you were ushering him into memory, that gossamer
afterlife. I could almost see you standing beside his grave:
        the headstones at Arlington like whitecaps

on a lake, your anguish coming in waves.... My sister claims
        that, given the chance, I'd push our pharaoh
in front of a bus. "He's getting old," she writes in an email.

"Have you no pity?" In the Egyptian *Book of the Dead*,
Ammit, the Devourer, awaits those whose hearts are out of balance.
    Let Ammit eat us unsentimentally. This world,
like the next, needs indigestible sorrow.... It's late in the third-set
    tiebreaker—the justice facing yet another

match point. A storm has taken the capital; the court's slick
    with reason. Though the trees tremble and the rains
pour down, the justice will not retire, the contest now like Canadian
    triples, what with that second Italian
aiding my father, swatting at balls, yelling, "Out! Out! Out!"
    There he is, the justice, moving wide
for a backhand, falling, slumping over. "God save the United
    States and this court!" mocks the litigator.

LESSONS

Like the song of the castrato
the blades of a helicopter—
their high-pitched whine
and whoosh

reaching not so much my ears
as my amygdalae. Almond
joy turns instantly
into terror.

My tennis lesson's husband,
who in summer shuttles
back and forth from
an eight-bedroom

"cottage" in Prouts Neck, Maine
to company headquarters
in Boston, is home,
and I am

in the shower with his silicon
trophy, Mrs. Backhand,
Mrs. Forehand, Mrs.
Lunging Volley.

Her will to improve, which
astonishes, depends on
two things: a legal,
teenage boy

like me and a new scoring
system. For now, what
must be added is
50-love.

Through the window, I watch
the Egyptian grass bow
down as the copter
lands on it,

and the husband, who favors
golf and who owns a major
league baseball team,
disembarks,

pausing for a moment to lap
up what is his—the great
water bowl of
the Atlantic.

The waves play fetch with
the rocky shore. Money
is the stick that keeps
them moving—

the view almost as fine as
the Winslow Homer
above the bed.
"Don't pull

out!" my lesson yells. "Don't you
dare pull out!" Odysseus,
I think, has returned
to slay

the teenage suitor. The spring
before, in Honors English,
I read about this
royal sailor.

Two decades older than his
bride, he now struggles
to stick the landing
of that other

craft, the one between his legs.
It used to steer him
to the bliss of
friendly

(and not so friendly) corporeal
takeovers. My fear balloons.
It's as if the copter's
come inside, its

rotors spinning furiously. Cuff-
linked Freddy Kruger's
on the stairs.
"I'm

almost there!" she cries. "He's
almost here!" I plead.
There, here; there,
here—like

some sort of frantic GPS or call-
and-response at church.
I'm Caffarelli nibbling
on my noble

lady's ear—or will be soon.
With my elongated limbs
and ribs, I look like
a tool

to pull up weeds. I'm a youthful
gardener planting seeds,
the water hitting my
back, beating

it silly. This Penelope is bad:
she's done no weaving
at all, and I love
her for it.

My mother's age exactly, though
distinctly not my mother,
she's like a mite once
trapped in

amber, free to trap herself.
And now I'm somehow
dressed and dripping
on the carpet.

"Darling, Ralph just helped me
with my backhand; he
mentioned that he
also plays

the clarinet." I mentioned nothing
of the sort. Handing me her
husband's instrument,
she says, winking,

"Play." The reed is dry, so very
dry. Reluctantly, I moisten
it, and then I dazzle
them, my

mother, for whom life is merely
something to survive, having
long ago decreed that I
take lessons.

This, friends, is privilege.

THE USES OF CATASTROPHE

*Washington is a sad city. It is depressed. It is stunned and it is cold and its
faith in the future is shaken. The economy is rotten and the federal
government is cutting back and unemployment has spread to white-collar
jobs and the Potomac River is a morgue for people who were heading for
the sun....*—Richard Cohen, the *Washington Post*

The 737 had an ice-tan. It lay too long on its black towel before taking off.
A minute later,

it dove into the 14th Street Bridge, flattening four cars, then fell, like Greg
Louganis,

into the Potomac. For a brief moment, the Air Florida jet's fractured
fuselage floated eerily

on the surface. Six ants fled the waterlogged carcass: five passengers and
a uniformed cherub—

upbeat altar girl for the once fussy (and now mostly dead) consumer. She
was floundering

in the frigid Potomac, having lost her poise, her marketing savvy, her
attention to the flight

attendant handbook. *We Move Our Tail for You!* The passengers clung to
the plane's behind,

like men who might never have sex again, their legs broken, their nearly
bankrupt bodies

losing heat faster than they could produce it. What sad, little factories!
They'd lost consciousness

colliding with the souls in front of them, and then, like newborns, had
come to

with a start, with a lung-contracting panic. When a gash appeared in
the watery limbo,

they had swum through it, the taste of jet fuel, that techno-meconium,
in their mouths.

**

What were they doing in the river, in our river, not six miles from the house,
those phantom

mendicants? "Go away!" I wanted to shout. "Don't encourage her!"
The *Special Report* arrived

like a subpoena from the Gods, cleaving mid-quarrel, mid-smooch,
the preposterous storyline

of an afternoon soap. YOU HAVE BEEN SERVED! And now my mother
would testify, would

talk again in tongues. "Yes, my husband was Achilles, the war criminal. Yes,
he brought the plane

down himself with a shoulder-fired missile. Yes, he belongs at The Hague
in a tiny glass box

devoured by tarantulas. Yes, the Potomac's complaint has merit." *My blue
watercourses back*

up, filled with dead; I cannot spend my current in the salt immortal sea,
being damned with corpses.

There was no finer witness to her own misery—she had not wanted to live
by my father,

which is to say she had not wanted to marry a river—than a flailing flight
attendant.

Coming to a theatre near us: a ready-made emblem for a stay-in-the-falls
mom. "Why isn't

anyone doing anything?" she said. "Jesus Christ! The woman needs help!"
And she did.

**

A giant hairdryer hovered in the sky, yet gave off no heat. The noise and
wind irritated

the trees. "Step out of the shower," it said. "Dry off." Had the trees not
been undergoing winter

chemo, they'd have styled their leaves in that voluminous feathered look
Farrah Fawcett made

famous. (Remember the poster that hung in my room: Angel of angels in
a red bathing suit,

all nipples and teeth.) The flight attendant was going under; she was too
weak to grab hold

of the Park Police helicopter's rope. The steer positively begged to be
lassoed. As a crowd gathered

on the Virginia bank, the news anchor climbed the ladders of consternation, strung pity

the way people string lights at Christmas (our tree was still up, though the Feast of the Three

Kings had passed). My mother donned a lifesaving wreath in solidarity. And then a burrowing animal,

a Congressional Budget Office gopher, waded out into the icy murk, as though digging a tunnel

of virtue under the White House lawn. "Her body just went limp," he would later say. "I think

she passed out…. Something told me to go in after her." Lenny Skutnick: A Hero of Our Time!

**

No, wait. That's a Russian reference and rather cynical—we can't have that. Brezhnev would soon blame

the crash on Reagan's dismantlement of PATCO. Reagan would soon wrest Mr. Skutnick away from my

mother who swooned over the man's mustached bravery—"He looks like Tom Selleck," she said.

What that teddy bear lacked in money he made up for in testosterone. A father of three who earned

$14,000 a year, he couldn't touch the tires—the luxury life rings—on my mother's Range Rover.

Nor could he play tennis. And yet with wrecks of fancy, it doesn't matter. They're a loan with

no money down; they're a home invasion by marching band—it's playing John Philip Sousa;

they're a thrill ride at an amusement park, a cognitive loop-the-loop—my stomach feels sick.

Two weeks later, Mr. Skutnick received an upgrade. A Republican gate agent had wanted to say, "Thank

you." At the high-flying State-of-the-Union address, he sat in first-class, next to Nancy Reagan who put

her hand on his knee when the President said, "Don't let anyone tell you that America's best

days are behind her. We've seen it triumph too often in our lives to stop believing now."

**

You have to be careful with china. It really needs to be cleaned by hand. That night, while soaking

dinner plates, my mother broke one and immediately stormed off in tears. The river in

our sink was warm and murky. Like Gulliver in Lilliput, I felt around the bottom, careful not

to disturb the bridge. A nearly perfect isosceles triangle poked through the suds. I lifted it

like a crane. Plastic army men—or maybe it was food—fought near
the drain, many of them

dead and moving toward it. (How I used to love the bath as a boy!) A
thousand homeless people

roved the streets, demanding life vests. By year's end, another million jobs
would be lost.

Soon, my mother would be heading for the sun—my parents had a condo
in Naples. Some screaming,

some fucking, some mixed doubles.... Soon the cherry blossoms would
mock democracy. Who can

abide their facile optimism? Even spring has its rhetoric. The commentators
applauded

the President's performance. It was as if he had risen from the mangled jet
himself. Nancy's smile spanned

the Potomac. You could drive a tank across it. And in her bedroom
balcony, I sat next to my own

**

first lady, holding her hand.

WATER PARK

I'm ascending with the other kids,
clutching my mat; twining upwards,
as on a church spire staircase;
twerking, as in a strip club

(I'm that excited)—
the three-foot wide pole
a steely god
as blue as my eyes and reaching,

it seems, into heaven.
Music beats the air—
the line frenetic yet orderly:
a caterpillar with two hundred brains,

each of them alert and dripping.
It's mid-July; the water park is packed.
It's like a suitcase,
which, having been hurled onto

a conveyor belt, bursts open.
Out scrambles all manner
of swimming trunks and bikinis,
all manner of skin....

Like drunken revelers,
my hormones jump
the line and begin coursing
through my body.

Suspiciously upbeat, even jovial,
my father has lifted martial law
and granted me some fun.
I want some fun, want it

desperately—as desperately
as I will search for lightbulbs
and a decent piece of meat
in 90s Poland. This scrap

of kindness comes as swiftly
as a punch to the back of my head.
The truth is, my father seeks
to punish my mother

who isn't feeling well,
who looks quite ghastly.
Pregnant with their fifth child,
she won't "just get rid of it."

And, hence, my strange happiness.
A girl in a bikini brushes my arm.
Sex, I think, is something that moves.
My mother stays put.

The sort of Catholic who says "no"
to salvation and "yes" to rules;
"no" to divorce and "yes," oh "yes,"
to black eyes and broken teeth,

she endures. She abides.
From atop the slide,
I can see her slumped over on a bench,
holding her stomach.

And then, suddenly, it's my turn.
On a flimsy rubber
mat, I plunge into fantasy,
trace the curves of a centerfold's

breasts, hips—
my body a five-foot, two-inch tongue,
darting in and out of her
looping, plastic mouth.

With a confidence borne of gravity,
I descend. I'm a sweet,
misogynistic avalanche—
the "a" in a girl's "I can't"

becoming the "u" in a boy's "You
cunt." It's a word my friends
have just begun to use.
Before I know it,

I finish in the grimy wading pool
of my groin. When I rub
the water from my eyes,
she is gone. I maneuver

frantically through the park
and find her in the Ladies' Room, moaning.
"Are you OK, Mom?" I ask,
cracking the door.

"Don't come in," she says.
This birthing into meanness,
into maleness…. The park
is more like a giant colon removing

waste than a woman's uterus.
Even now, hearing the word "miscarriage,"
I remember the rapid, wet-luge
corkscrew of want.

"THE LADY CRAZIES"

For the Honorable Brett Kavanaugh

All of Washington is
on the move, every

meowing uterus, every
convent clogged

with venomous
semen. The body

politic shakes,
as though having

a seizure. Each
womb inches forward,

pushes up,
as in a packed

Metro, jostling
her viscera.

"Make room, make
room," the conductor

cries.
Senator bees apply

honey to the nation's
vaginas. They can't

help but sting
the hysterical

patients. The White
House chef

stuffs garlic into
their mouths—clove

after clove. "I can't
breathe! I can't

breathe!" The uteri
retreat, like old-

fashioned vampires,
repelled by one

scent, lured by
another.

Soon, they're
recaptured

and put in
their place,

like a girl at a party
thrown onto a

bed or a woman
at a hearing

thrown out with
the truth.

LITTLE FALLS

1.

The deadliest spot on the entire
Potomac—far deadlier
than Great Falls, Virginia
whose chutes and rapids

were like some tantruming diva
from whom the sensible knew
to keep their distance
and, from a distance,

enjoyed the eruptive spectacle.
The star of our backyard production
was imperceptibly difficult
and self-regarding—

her show more *Sesame Street*
than *Bluebeard's Castle*.
A mere five-foot drop,
as innocuous as any playground

slide, then open water.
Who could be afraid of that?
History's baby pool,
history's foaming crib—

fifteen drowned in as many years.
With a name like "Little Falls,"
you'd think the river itself
was in love with irony

(that ambush we moderns can't ever
seem to get enough of). Here's
the story I used to tell myself.
I tell it tonight while watching the tube,

reports of atrocity on the crawl:
24 UNARMED IRAQIS SHOT DEAD.
COVER-UP BEGINS TO UNRAVEL....
When Agnes stormed the capital

in June of 1972, a wrathful girl
returned to punish Rome,
her chastity preserved,
her disgust at power's arrogance

become ungovernable, a nuisance
in heaven (the Watergate break-in
had just occurred), she got ahold
of the dam behind our house,

and, in her fury, opened up a cavern
beneath the falls: a swirling pit
of rock and debris into which
even the most competent sportsman

could be sucked, then spit out
a day, a week, sometimes a month, later.
Our dog would usually find the bodies.
One, a marine, had been entirely

relieved of his face—
prepared, as dead soldiers ought to be,
for the future's inattention.
Round and round, he'd gone

in that indifferent agitator,
trying, I almost want to say, to get clean,
to crawl back inside the womb,
his skull worn smooth

by the jagged concrete
(our spa's most aggressive exfoliant).
And what were his crimes, this soldier
out on a lovely Sunday afternoon,

this soldier robbed of more
than his uniform?
He was too young for My Lai
and too old for Haditha.

2.

Once, in a rented canoe, my father
tried to cross the Potomac.
(Think of him as a less noble
George Washington.)

From the bank, "The Last-of-
Many-Straws"—my mother—
begged him not to.
"Please!" she cried, "Please!"

as he paddled at an angle
slightly up-river. She'd run down
after him, falling twice on the path,
certain he would drown.

The current was particularly strong
that day, and the pickpocket shadows
moved sideways through the elms.
By this point, the Park Police

had installed a cable above the falls,
the entire width of the Potomac,
so that people might grab hold
of it as they went over.

"The world doesn't want for fools,"
a police spokesman said.
Translation: *If it kills you,*
they will come. In lieu of a net,

into which an aerialist might fall
and pleasantly laugh at her mistake,
a line in the sandy sky between life
and death. If you held onto it

until the helicopter came, you just
might hang a chance.
No matter the signs that for a mile
said, "Go back! Go back!

Dangerous Falls ahead!"
When for a moment, my father
stopped paddling—was he tired
or simply taunting his adversary?—

the Last-of-Many-Straws yelled,
"I could have had anyone I wanted!"

"Anyone" meant the last Giant
to strike out in the '51 World Series.

She'd been drinking, her words
were like spray on the rocks
and just as slurred as the river's.
If you listen, the drowned

will try to tell you their story:
Girl Scout cover girl of New York City…
early TV game show assistant….
"Fuck you, you bastard!"

she screamed. Even in her
wedding photos, she seemed sad.
All lace, thin, beautiful.
With the words "I do,"

a thousand dreams had cascaded
from the ledge of her mouth.
I pictured my father hanging
from the cable (as I had once

in a dream), like a fly to sticky paper:
defiant, not wanting help from anyone,
least of all the government.
A self-made amphibian, adaptable,

adept everywhere (bravado, his arms;
hubris, his lungs). He was
only thirty yards from the falls,
not halfway across the Potomac,

when a much less dismissible tongue
nearly devoured him. I paddled
with my eyes, half-hoping
for a rapid comeuppance.

3.

The Potomac doesn't care. A bad
government? A bad marriage? Soldiers
broken like matchsticks, going off
like improvised explosive devices?

It yawns at human villainy
or, like the elderly at a matinee,
sleeps right through the film. Little
Falls, that lazy fox, lounges in wait.

The unsuspecting come directly to it.
Why expend energy? Why make any
distinctions at all between the deserving
and undeserving? Remain in your den,

Mr. Fox; you will get fed one way
or another. From the current's
perspective, we are all just loosened
teeth in the mouth of time.

The rich, with any luck, stay in place.
After seven or eight decades, they fall out.
The poor find pliers in the dental dark.
The black and brown are pulled,

over and over. ("Get out of your car!")
Yesterday, I watched four geezers play tennis.
They couldn't move, though they were
no doubt pretty good in their youth.

They joked, cursed, got a little testy,
as former titans of industry will do.
After they were done, one swept
the Har-Tru court; another cleaned the lines.

Not a single trace of their encounter
remained. I shouldn't feel pity for them,
I really shouldn't, but I do.
One winter, a giant sheet of ice,

as big as a failing mall's parking lot,
went over the dam. It had
been stuck, the river moving
beneath it with great pressure,

when suddenly the mirror lurched
and then shattered in the water
below. The cavern coughed up
bits of glass for days.

COLLEGE TRIP

He's like an ATM
in a rainstorm,
spitting out money—
so much wet dough,
so many smackers—
then gobbling it
back up again.

Or he's like a cow
in the long green,
the whispering fields
of moolah. Corporate
America's kinky ruminant
chewing—no, licking—
his cud.

This man is my father.
I'd throw up if I weren't
already doing so.
I have the stomach flu.
I'm moaning softly;
he's moaning loudly.
We're a veritable chorus.

Talk about irrational
exuberance!
(Where is Alan Green-
span when you need him?)
My father might as well
be Tony Soprano who
used his daughter's

college trip
to whack a rival.
The room shrinks
to the size of his 911
Porsche.
It rounds a curve,
and I wretch.

We're parallel lines
with no transversal—
one pleasure, one
pain—a diseased
geometry.
The wastebasket takes
my temperature;

the curtains bring
me a glass of water.
The next day,
I offend the very sandals—
and toes!—
of the Williams College
interviewer.

On the floor: my gross
domestic product.
A chunk of ill-digested
sausage glares
at me.
As I leave,

I hear the interviewer
say to a colleague,

"What a nervous
young man!"
I won't get in,
won't ever get out
of that gas-pedal
room.

THE COLUMNIST

1. Scare Course I

What is a chickenhawk? Well, I am not talking about a bird or a cartoon character. A chickenhawk is someone who beats the drums of war; someone willing to send others off to fight and die in wars when they, themselves, have never served in uniform.—Henrietta Bowman

Who says poetry makes nothing happen?
    Neither flaccid on war nor flaccid on etymology, he got paid
for putting words in Tricky Dick's mouth: a gig—or is it a gag?—
    that still gets him off.
The great contrarian apologist for scoundrels of a conservative bent,

    Arch-fiend Lucifer's witty lieutenant
who somehow excused himself *Before the Fall.*
    Ever since, he's made of language a correctional facility,
a Federal pen, a war zone—flying in on Sunday mornings,
    like Dubya to Baghdad, to rally his lexicographical troops

and reserve grammarians. Scare Course I
    having to land on an unlit page, its own lights turned low
for fear of anti-prose craft missiles.
    So much bravado! The columnist in the mess hall
of human history. His troops still smarting

    from a string of losses: rocket-propelled run-ons,
improvised explosive fragments, not to mention
    subject-verb disagreements of a neo-colonial variety.
And all around, whispers of a pointless war.
    "Language on!" he exhorts his fellow chickenhawks.

2. Touring Talent

*When I was writing witty put-downs of the left-stooping media…in the
late 60's and early 70's…I was convinced the red snide…would be
turned back and a new era of enlightened government stewardship by
well-meaning, if somewhat flawed, rich white men would stay the course
of this country. And then those bungling idiots made a little too much
noise at Larry O'Brien's and it took eight years, and a well-timed
hostage crisis, to right the ship of state.*—William Safire

I sing of the columnist's son who sang with me
    in a barbershop quartet called "The Bearitones"—
that's B-E-A-R-itones (our high school mascot was the bears;
    hence, the neon pun). We were, you'll forgive me,
truly unbearable, even on our hind legs

    and with our eyeteeth flashing.
Like politicians who can't stay on message, we couldn't stay on key—
    not for the life of us (nor, alas, for the death of our prey).
"It's the harmony, stupid! The harmony!"
    Four rich kids trying to get into college,

we'd donated our services to an organization named
    "Touring Talent," which provided uplift
to old folks' homes and state mental hospitals—
    holiday *sneer*, as one of us put it back then.
The columnist must have scoffed at the highly regulated markets

    of adolescent upward mobility.
Down with betterment programs! Down with compulsory volunteerism!
    But he had to have understood his child's advantage:
how much easier for a private school kid to appear
    more socially concerned

than for a public school one to appear more academically prepared—
    the latter like the inferior goods of a crumbling,
state-run industry in need of the Iron Lady's fist.
    "Relax," he might have told himself, "it's a virtue-
for-profit venture, one sure to pay off in the long run,

    what with the value of an Ivy League degree."
On weekends, we Bearitones performed as backup singers
    for a rock band—thoughts of college admission
(and Alzheimer's patients) far from our minds.
    It was art for art's sake, compassion on holiday.

One particular Saturday night, we set up in an abandoned lot
    in Georgetown, between a bank
and a Chinese restaurant. Before the cops came to shut us down,
    we had a pretty good groove going:
a crowd of maybe a hundred applauding and dancing

    to our version of "Twist and Shout."
As back-up singers we couldn't do that much damage
    to the melody, and what damage we could do
our equipment kindly obscured. The party platform:
    "It's the noise, stupid! The noise!"

A few days later, the columnist shocked us all by mentioning
    the concert in one of his columns. He wrote
of the "gathering multitudes at M Street and Wisconsin"—
    the voice half-Ed Sullivan, half-*Old Testament* prophet.
It seemed a plug any band would die for.

    We were seventeen and in the *New York Times*!
But you could tell from the tone how much he disdained
    popular culture. (Where some band members

saw a laurel, I saw a noose, hyperbole's hangman.)
　　Moreover, the prig hadn't actually heard us sing,

not in either of our incarnations. How tempting
　　to think of the gesture as a touching betrayal
of aesthetic principles, a father's love winning out at last
　　but in a currency, a *tender* shall we say,
that no discerning treasury could recognize? What?

　　To be written about with the same corrosive sarcasm
the man reserved for Democrats? Recently, the columnist
　　has endeavored to be more genuine,
praising the 43rd President's "moving exposition of the noble goals
　　of American foreign policy" and adding,

for his readers' edification, "A carefully constructed speech,
　　like a poem or a brief or a piece of music,
has a shape that helps make it memorable."
　　(When he speaks of a "piece of music," he isn't,
I assure you, thinking of "Twist and Shout.")

　　This gem of the first water is only too thankful
to have witnessed the second restoration of Republican valor.
　　And all it took was some hanging chads
and a partisan court to usher in an age of militaristic sincerity.
　　The red snide gone, the blue snide having found

a candidate who so butchers the language
　　he must be genuine—stupidity having become a kind
of messianic movement. ("Does anybody here speak English?"
　　a public school kid cries, his unarmored Humvee in flames,
his comrade bleeding on the ground.) So what

if the columnist betrays his own intelligence?
After all, the ventriloquist gets to manipulate the dummy.
Cheer up, poor reader, the columnist has also lived
to see his son become a populist. The alumni magazine reports
my former classmate is now

"Director of User Experience Research" at a computer firm.
His job: "usability improvement,"
the Arthurian "quest for a user-friendly screen."
O, Guinevere, can life really offer up such ironies?
The son of the Usage Czar wanting to make communication

easier for the common practitioner?
What next? A virtual egalitarianism? But lest anyone imagine
too much conflict in the Safire household,
I should confess that my classmate's also grown up to be
a rich white man, that most bipartisan of achievements.

I know. Who am I to talk? Who am I to write poetry?
What does it matter if sons rebel?
What of that rebellion? I, for instance, am the most nostalgic
and ineffectual of things: a left-stooping academic.
(As my father once quipped, "Those who can, screw;

those who can't, preach.")
This afternoon, listening to the columnist blather on
about the upcoming election,
I was reminded of the time we Bearitones were heckled
during a Touring Talent performance.

An old man with stringy hair, in a wheel chair, dentures
literally in hand, shouted, "I won't listen to this!
I've had enough!" While trying to keep the base line going,

the columnist's son whispered, "Just keep singing.
Just keep singing." And we did—

until the man was removed.

II

The world is a fine place. The only thing wrong with it is us.

—Anton Chekhov, Letter to A.S. Suvorin

PATTI DAVIS IS MY HERO

You were quite
young, just 24, when
you took matters

into that most
intimate of voting
booths: your womb.
The affairs of State
were personal;
your tubal ligation,

elective. A
genetic Benedict
Arnold,

you renounced the Reagan-
Davis line. You
felled the family
tree like
a callow George
Washington.

Hollywood was
your Ticonderoga—
or did it capture

you? Darling
of the Left, you were
like toilet paper:
to be used.

Any party would
do.

Hope, let us say, is
sometimes surgical,
sometimes self-

destructive. It
always wears a mask.... I,
too, vowed never to
procreate, never
to permit my
own replication.

Genes are
like radon in
the basement.

Instead, I adopted a
six-year-old boy
from foster care
whose alcoholic mother
your father called
a "welfare queen."

In heaven
she drives a
Cadillac.

My parents were appalled.
"You come from such
good stock," my
mother said, whose

mother, a cleaning lady,
died on her knees.

It was like letting the
yard man swim
in the pool.

Still worse, the boy had
a disability and his father
had AIDs—what Pat Buchanan,
White House
Communications Director,
dubbed "nature's

revenge on gay
men and drug
addicts."

Your father might as well
have been a Trappist
monk for all he
said—a monk who
makes honey
and coffins.

The nouveau riche
can't afford to be
merciful. Nor

can a battered woman.
Another's pain, even
a small neglected
child's, asks too much

of her. It arrives like
an accusation.

It arrives like an
unpaid bill or lien
on the future.

Ten years after tying
that knot, you
untied it, Patti—or
had it untied. You
would now husband
possibility,

though your
mother, you would
later say,

lived deep inside you.
A Sicilian monster
lives deep inside
me. I see him
in my own fits of
anger.

A tumor in
the brainstem,
he can't be

excised. When
the Dutchman commenced
his "long goodbye," you
commenced to melt,

like the Greenland
ice sheet—

the first sign
of a global
warming.

His Alzheimer's you
called a "pirate
disease"—each memory
a ship that is
plundered and set
on fire. Yet,

there was no
more convincing
Captain Hook

than your father.
He made the poor
and least among us
walk the plank.
In fact, he did it with
a smile. During

his Hollywood
days, he fed
suspected Reds

to Hoover's crocodiles.
I find that
informative…. In
the end, you

took pity on your
parents. Death, you

understood, is an
old-fashioned
Bolshevik:

unyielding, un-
sympathetic, it lines
up each of us against
a wall. Sometimes
the bullet moves
quickly; sometimes

it inches along.
(With your father,
we all scream,

"Tear down that
wall!") Was it
wisdom, Patti, or
a failure of nerve
that other thing
growing inside you?

My son wants
nothing to do with
his birth

family. Not even his
sister who took
care of him
when their mother

was drunk or stoned
or selling her

body. I've taught
that boy what
I could.

RIVER PORN

Alexander Haig has come to see the house!
Alexander Haig has come to see the house!
Have I told you that Alexander Haig has come to see

the house? Tired of the same old spread,
my father's put his peep show on the market,
and now the former Secretary,

having just been through it,
wants to look more closely at the river.
(A cool five million, and he gets the girl for good.)

The realtor thinks it ill-advised—what
with the copperheads and steep embankment.
But the former Secretary insists.

"I'm in charge. I'm in charge," he shouts.
He's like the guy who has to cross the line at strip shows,
the guy who has to touch the dancers. In the end,

he's like the old man with the prostitute
who can't get out of bed—literally.
His wife is pulling on his arm; the realtor's

pushing from behind, and still they can't ascend.
"A home like this should have a cable car," he whines—
his wife and realtor panting.

(A home like this should have a Sandinista son.)
Hiding in the attic, with the window cracked,
I'm oddly heartened that my father's house

might have the ultimate Good News Lord.
The river—meanwhile—slips and falls.
No, she's bending into Washington.

AS FRANK CARLUCCI LAY DYING

Not so much Christ walking on water as Patrice Lumumba coming out of it,
    rising like mist—a dark cloud.
Not so much Patrice Lumumba in swimming trunks as Patrice Lumumba
    in that other kind of suit,
    preparing a statement, an angry one.
    The words are like fish; they leap from the page.
Not so much Patrice Lumumba at the Congolese shore, frolicking in
    the surf, as Patrice Lumumba in our nation's capital,
    begging for help.
    Belgian troops will support the coup....
Patrice Lumumba on the Patawomeck,
Patrice Lumumba on the Patawomeck,
    your side of the Patawomeck or River of Swans.

Say his name, Frank. He's about to knock on your front door,
    every last moldering bit of him.
When you coughed, the falls coughed, too, and out popped Patrice
    Lumumba, history's inconvenient hope—
    like a piece of meat
    or a small tree stuck in the river's throat.
"The only thing we wanted for our country is the right to a worthy life,
    to dignity without pretense,
    to independence without restrictions."
Patrice Lumumba, pan-Africanist, post-colonialist, who dared to ask
    the Soviets for help.
There he is on your tennis court, taking down the net.
    No more backhands, Frank, no more forehands, no more
    serving the elite.

You were second secretary in the Congo—in other words,
    a CIA operative—

not so much a lover of freedom as a pitiless pragmatist
  and Cold War veteran.
(*My Neighbor, the Assassin*—that's what I called you, though you denied
  any involvement
  and didn't do the deed yourself.)
President Eisenhower had said to Allen Dulles, "Patrice Lumumba must
  be eliminated."

And now he's standing in your bedroom, talking to your wife,
  dripping on the Persian carpets.
Patrice Lumumba wants a word with you, a few minutes
  of your time,
  though you don't have many minutes left.
Is this a dream? A reckoning? There's nothing you can give Patrice
  Lumumba, Frank.
  Even "tough, little monkeys," as your father described you, die.
After all these years, Patrice will take you to the afterlife
  in his shackled arms.

DRAIN ENTRAPMENT INCIDENT

The problem is to connect, without hysteria, the pain
of anyone's body with the pain of the world's body.
—Adrienne Rich

That's what
the paper called it when
a girl, charmed by the frothing
water, was drawn down into
a spa and deprived
of oxygen.

Virginia Graeme
Baker, only seven years
old, the former Secretary of
State's granddaughter—
her body made
the perfect

seal, though
not the kind that swims
or sings. Her mother followed
her by vowing to get
to the bottom
of things.

Grief, of course,
has no bottom; it's just
a kind of sewerage, a dentist
saying, "Suction, please."
And now her baby's
in her mouth,

that other tub
that spits and gurgles—
she's a tooth that won't come
out.... After the lawsuit
and the lobbying,
a bill

to protect
the smallest of
consumers, a bill in Virginia's
name. (That of a parrot,
let us say, or Northern
Shoveler—how

she loved
her animals!) The bill
was championed by her gramps
who had once forged an
international coalition:
a many-jetted

enterprise
and waterfall of tears:
sortie after sordid.... Children
schooled by errant smart
bombs; Iraqi
soldiers

plowed under
in the desert—they, too,
couldn't breathe. (Feel the sand;
it's like a dentist's toothpaste
on your tongue.) Once
the manufacturer

stopped
blowing bubbles at
the Bakers, the fix was simple:
a drain with a curved cap on
it, like half a pumpkin
or the dome

of St. Peter's
Basilica. The seal is
not exact this way; a child can
pretend to be a water
sprite or lily pad.
In dreams

sometimes, I
correct the past, as if
it were a student paper. Virginia:
too young for history, though
not for wealth. She's like
Jacques Cousteau

exploring
a deep sea thermal vent,
or she's like Atlas, not so much
holding up the world
as trying somehow
to hug it.

MEMORIAL DAY, 1990

On America's Failed Free Verse Invasion of the Underworld

From a distance, it must have all
seemed quite feasible: no
anti-tank helicopters, no
fighter jets, no
surface-to-air-missiles.
An entire country,
an entire theme,
left entirely unprotected—
as if to mock, the President
believed, his heartfelt
intentions.

> *The dead must not be forced*
> *to cross the River Styx!*
> ("Does he mean Panama, Nicaragua,
> or Chile?" whispered
> the Secretary of Defense.)
> *No one should have to taste*
> *the sweet waters of oblivion.*
> *Call it "Operation We*
> *Shall Never Forget!"*
> *Our mission is to sink the ferry;*
> *to kidnap General Charon,*
> *that pock-marked, bribe-taking,*
> *drug-running necrophiliac;*
> *to overthrow his government.*
> *American deaths,* he told
> the audience, *depend on it!*

Repeat after me:
"The belly-up want free, fair,
and credible elections!
The belly-up want free, fair...."

In the mountains above the Styx,
in the jungles,
and in the dark, roiling river itself,
our Poet-in-Chief suffered
a tremendous beating.
The dead did not rise
up in revolt;
the ferry, more rickety skiff
than battleship,
could not—
cannot?—be sunk.
The dead, he now says,
will be led by anyone.

Each day these lowlifes arrive
with money in their mouths,
at first shocked, and then appalled,
by their apparent consciousness.
I say, "Let the dead forget!"

"Do you still believe
in poetry?" a reporter asks,
"or solemnity?"

Read my lips:
no new elegies!
Next question.

"Was this a failure
of American Intelligence
or American Empathy?"

> *For too long we have served*
> *as the world's hippocampus.*
> *The era of memory building is over!*
> Having turned on a dime
> and spinning like
> an Iowa weathervane,
> the President adds,
> with calculated petulance,
> *Why should* we *have to do*
> *the dead's remembering?*

FEBRUARY SOJOURN

For Abeer Qassim Hamza al-Janabi, 14

The snow, that soiled dress,
lies strewn along the highway.
Some god has had his fun
at winter prom.

The car allows for one long
replay of the violence,
the windows like a TV screen
or soldier's mind.

Say the girl from Mahmoudiya wasn't raped.
Say her sister wasn't shot.
Say Spring's an unrepentant sophist—
all daffodils and sun.

Who can absorb the horror
three continents away?
Who now   sips,   sips,   sips
his sympathetic latte,

which, perched beside the radio,
gives up all its warmth
like a body far too generous,
a girl become the land?

THE SLEEPING SENTINEL

1.

Long after the 3rd Vermont Infantry
moved south to Camp Lyon
in Alexandria, Virginia,
I move north.

We are not so much ships crossing
in the ahistorical night as
demented, migratory
birds. I've

abandoned my post, given up guarding
the Potomac. My time as
a sentry, I decided,
was over.

I will no longer defend the union
of marital woe and drowning,
iniquitous Republicans and
fatherhood. Like

Private William Scott of Groton, I was
tired. I was hungry. Tiny, disease-
ridden vampires made love
to my limbs.

Their whining sounded like an orchestra
of unchanged diapers tuning itself.
Mud was everywhere: on my
shoes, in my mouth.

"Let the Confederate troops storm
the capital!" I said to myself.
"Let the wooden planks
of Chain Bridge

feel the hooves of a thousand horses!"
I would rather see all the snow
that ever fell in Vermont
than to endure

the weather we have to endure here.
But now, as I reach St. Johnsbury,
truth presents itself
like a plate

of food: I am the *enemy*. My parents,
with their talk of "spooks"
and "Canadians"
(as a child,

how could I have known that the latter
was code for Jews?), morph
into Jefferson Davis
and his first

wife, Sarah Taylor, who died after three
months of marriage—beaten
savagely by malaria
(my mother

has always been something of a ghost). Fact:
I lived on the Dixie side of the river.
How could this have
escaped me?

Fact: my uniform was grey, not blue. Fact:
my heart is as green as a hundred
dollar bill—as green as the grass
above my grave.

2.

Another dream. In this one, Bowe Bergdahl
gives it a rest—Vermont, after all, is
not Afghanistan—and I
become Private

Scott himself. The two "D"s, desertion
and dereliction, are my only
available fates. Asleep,
my mind

flies like a bat through centuries; awake,
it hangs from the cable above
the falls or in that sloshing
cavern below

them. I've been sentenced to death.
Apparently, the future of
Washington depends
on two eyelids.

Like flags, they drop through no fault
of their own. They fight for an
insomniac general
whose horse

hasn't eaten in months. The battlefield
is bloodshot. Would that my pupils
were Caesar and my eyelashes,
palm fronds!

No one likes the early autumn heat. Even
at night, it slaps the great rump of
the Capital. I languish less
than a mile

from where I'll languish 125 years hence—
somehow in the dream I know this.
The boys have petitioned
General "Baldy,"

that cannon of mercy. My hands and feet
are tied. I can feel the rough brick
of the wall behind me. Twelve
rifles take aim at my

chest, and I soil my pants. I shake across time.
Then, as in a movie, I'm granted a last-
second reprieve: Honest Abe has
a weakness for sons.

3.

When my father travels to the White House
to thank the President personally, he is
aloof and arrogant. He declines
the money

that Lincoln tries to give him in recognition
of his sacrifice. The War has robbed
his farm of familial hands—
cut them off

and sent them south. To the corn and cows,
the fields might as well be a graveyard.
And soon they'll be just that: all
four sons in uniform;

all four.... My father has other ideas;
he wants to do some business
with the man from Illinois.
He's like Trump's

children in Moscow, playing *Let's Make
Them Kneel.* Let's make them lick
Putin's shoe. ("Come on,
now, PUT

the toe IN your mouth!") My dreams are
irresponsible: they feast, like a mule,
on rotten hay bales of
anachronism.

In five months' time, the Great Emancipator
will lose a second son—I see the boy
at the top of the Grand
Staircase; he's

already in decline. My father waves at him.
And then I'm running toward the rifle
pits at Lee's Mills, grateful for
a second, more

honorable chance at death. Lincoln, ever
dignified, bows his bloody head.
A curtain comes down
on all of us....

4.

In this dream, my mother rises like a duck
at a carnival show: she will not be shot
like that. She will not—again
and again. Her

son Robert Todd Lincoln, who looks suspiciously
like my brother James, has ushered her
into a private asylum in
Batavia. She's

been acting erratically, spending money
again. She wants to redecorate
the small mansion of her
skull.

The antiques, sadly, prove fraudulent;
the draperies, much too big for her
eyes. Robert Todd—my
brother—runs

a *Fortune 500* company; it's the Amazon.com
of home furnishings. He, too, has lost
a son—his, to brain cancer.
With respect

to women's health, the man wields the power
of the purse with a Dartmouth smile;
he's a congress of one.
Unlike Mary

Lincoln, whose brothers fought and died
for the Confederacy, my mother
will never get out. When she
says, as she did once

in life, "The people here are very interesting.
At last, I have someone to talk to," all
of the furniture in Heaven
begins to sob.

WHEN I WAS A TENNIS PRO

I loved George Bush.
There, I said it.
Not the son, never
the son.
41, who fell
from the sky
into the anything
but pacific Pacific.
Ellen DeGeneres
shouldn't be
generous,
and nor should I,
who would gun
down flies,
those black, slow-
moving bombers
of Southern Maine,
with merely
a racket.
As Woody Guthrie
would say,
"These strings
kill fascists."
("Whack it!" I'd
yell, "before
it takes out
your carrier arm.")
My charges?
Old women as big
as barges—

cramped in
their panties.
The courts,
like the Panama
Canal, would have
to be widened—
or shrunk.
"Skunk! Skunk!"
My badgers
couldn't move,
but boy
were they ready
with expensive
perfume.
"What can I spray?"
Fact is: the Vice
was nice.
The Vice was Yale.
A genteel eel,
a prudent rudent,
a rat rarely unkind
or ungracious,
he was, I admit, a bit
of a racist—well,
more than a bit,
though Willie
Horton hadn't yet
happened (or
maybe I should
say, hadn't yet
crappened?).
The man's very
initials would

suggest both path
and prize.
George did—God
less him—what
Ronald said:
he served
only second serves;
never seemed
too able,
too powerful,
too much
in command.
There, at hand,
at club, he was,
flanked by
creepy perverts
(the secret service),
all trench coats
and guns.
He'd come to bat
the ball around
with friends,
fellow Oil Men,
big spends
who, like dentists,
loved to drill.
Call them Money
Mouths; call them
Honey Pumpers.
Their spirits were
crude; their
manners, refined.
The assigner of courts

was 18-year-old I.
The perverts
insisted that
Vice be moved
from Court 1
to Court 6,
a place more
protected,
where pines
collected.
The view there
of the water
was worse;
the view there
of the water
un-hearsed.
A sniper would
have a much
harder time.
But my badgers
refused: my badgers
who couldn't, now
wouldn't, move.
They'd played on
Court 6 for
half a century.
Mondays at 10:00
were theirs.
The court was
reserved—like
property, conserved.
No sentry would
boot them.

Vice was elastic;
Vice was fantastic.
"Let death come
by lob or
lobsterman,"
he joked.
"Court 1 is fine.
Court 5, Court 3—
wherever you
wish." And then
he winked at me,
foreseeing my pain
and diminished
pockets had I
forced the barges
to flee.
A country-club
prophet, he
instantly got it,
and fed me
some kindness
from a Sterling
spoon.
I wept while
watching his funeral.
Even in death
he seemed
smooth—buffed
like a banister
(to where?).
His children
loved him;
his grandkids cried,

"Poppy!"
O Lord was I
sloppy with
my thinking
and feels.

GO TO HELL, ROBERT MUELLER

He looks for evidence
of Russian influence
on my poetry.

He says that Pushkin,
Turgenev, and
Chekhov

ran a web brigade—
a troll farm—in
St. Petersburg.

That they turned America
toward my work
unnaturally.

I've never met these men.
I don't even read
poetry; I just

write it. *My hands are*
normal hands.
The five

fingers represent
the five key
factors

every entrepreneur
dreaming of
success

must master. How many
times do I have to
say it? No

collusion! None. Nada.
And the Steele
Dossier,

that fake news filth?
It puts me in bed
with Anna

Akhmatova. Never heard
of her. Never been
to Moscow.

Never been to grief. *Wild*
honey smells of
freedom

The dust—of sunlight
The mouth of a
young girl,

like a violet, but gold—
smells of nothing.
What the hell

does that mean? Gold
smells of power!
It's perfect

on a toilet seat. Even
better on a cock
ring.

I fired the Poet General
because he wouldn't
rhyme.

The guy's writing sucks.
He wasn't up to
the job,

OK? I did everyone
a favor. My only
fault, which

isn't a crime—in fact,
it's perfectly
legal—is

the obstruction of hope,
the obstruction of
beauty.

THE MAN WHO CARED ABOUT HIS TEETH

1.

They say that a drowning man clutches at a straw and that he has not
enough presence of mind at the time to grasp that while a fly may ride
the straw, his ten or twelve stone will not; but the idea does not occur
to him at the time and he goes on clutching at the straw.
  –Nikolai Gogol, *Dead Souls*, Part I

He waits in the waiting room, nose in a book:
        Dead Souls, Part I. He reads Gogol in
                the office, Gogol in the barn,

Gogol at the beach. He recalls "The Nose,"
        a tale about a man who's lost
                his nose. "Let us sniff

around the similes," he says. A crab and a bat
        and a beautiful, golden carriage....
                A fly in the soup, cancer

in the gut—his teeth need fixing, regardless.
        Neglected teeth will pine for a dentist.
                As in a room, a tiny room

marked *For Interrogations*, his head back,
        his mouth irradiated, he wholeheartedly
                concedes hygienic depravity:

a large garden of plaque—"My, my!"—two
        broken caps—"Look at this!"—gums
                as swollen as a sated leech.

A white-robed woman cleans his smoke-
    stained teeth, gives him a sermon
        on fluoride and flossing

and on the existence of hope, somewhere.
    A needle penetrates his gum.
        ("Somewhere?

Wheresome?") He thinks of Gogol foraging
    a snuff-box without the aid of
        fingers; Gogol caning

the life out of sunning, Swiss lizards; "Gogol,"—
    the needle penetrates again—"is
        that your nose or

are you eating a banana?" He clings to the
    Russian proverb: *The man with the*
        longest nose sees further.

2.

...not unlike a drowning man unexpectedly reappearing on the surface amid the joyful shouts of the crowd gathered on the bank of a river. But vainly do his brothers and sisters throw a rope into the river and wait for the drowning man's back or exhausted arms to appear again.
—Nikolai Gogol, *Dead Souls*, Part II

At home he lies in bed, long nose in a long
    book: *Dead Souls*, Part II. The
        months pass, the leaves

turn, his hair falls out. But how he learns to
  relish the habitual joy of brushing;
    the feel of the floss as

it glides between his teeth, removing all (and
  only all) that is unnecessary and
    harmful. How he

talks of Gogol on a hunger strike, his frail
  body carried to the baths; Gogol
    with half a dozen leeches

dangling from his nose; Gogol moaning as the
  leeches fall into his mouth. How
    he takes satisfaction

in his mouth's improvement, dealing out
  cash to have the root canals done,
    the fillings, the caps.

After a while, he even says to himself, "My
  smile's come back!" He sits
    facing the water—

white coats around him like snowflakes or
  angels—everything smelling of
    Gogol: Gogol's headlong

quest to find a moral for his story; Gogol
  hatching an epic—Part II? Part
    III?—and losing his nose;

Gogol, in a last glimmer of light, burning half
    of *Dead Souls*. "So you're off
        playing hearts with

the man next door! Suit yourself!" he cries
    to a nurse. "My nose, mind my
        nose!" And yet, even

deluged with delirium, he looks at himself
    in the mirror, not noticing the
        weight-loss, the fact

that his hair has fallen out, his scars like
    petunias. He notices only his teeth,
        his impossibly white teeth.

84

The word *father*
is the spent shell
of a peanut

or the husk of sweet
corn in July.
No, that's not right.

The word *father*
is a parachute
that will not open,

no matter how
gently—or ferociously—
you pull the cord.

I'm allergic to peanuts
and so very scared
of heights.

The word *father*
is a child
in the wood-paneled,

5-door wayback
of time.
He sits facing

the past,
counts the miles
until he might

be loved.
"Are we there yet, Dad?
Are we there?"

The word *father*
is an enzyme that dissolves
longing.

Or maybe it's lye on
a murder victim.
Come lye with me,

the years say.
The wagon's become
a rocket;

the boy, an astronaught.
Not much farther, not
much father....

Eat your peanuts, Ralph.
Pull the fucking
cord!

O CALVIN, O CALVIN

A president so sour and uncommunicative—
"He looks as though he has been weaned
on a pickle," quipped Alice Longsworth,
eldest daughter of rough swinging

Teddy Roosevelt, who built the first
White House tennis court,
a rolled dirt affair costing $2000
and sitting where presidents now serve

in the full-moon obtrusion that has
come to symbolize the presidency.
The court lasted only seven years
before Howard Taft, who much preferred

golf, ploughed it under (at 300 pounds,
he could barely move). The second court
lasted a good deal longer: long enough
for the sons of "Silent Cal"—a man,

went the joke, of two words ("You lose")—
to play tennis on it; long enough
for one of them, Calvin Junior,
to develop a blister on his big toe—

he should have been wearing socks;
long enough for the infection to travel
throughout his body, as though by train,
the way his father had from Vermont

upon hearing of Warren Harding's death.
What a great country the human form is—
and its capital the little mount heart....
I try to picture Calvin Senior in the White

House garden: helpless, distraught, desperate
to do something, anything really, as his son
begins to fade. And so, he catches a rabbit
and brings it to Calvin Junior's room.

Perhaps death, that other wordless thing,
can be distracted; perhaps it can even
be delighted. The animal quivers;
its delicate eyes beg for mercy. If love

is a magician, then maybe it can pull
a sixteen-year-old boy from the day's dark
top hat. He'd send in the navy if he could.
The U.S.S. *Penicillin*! It isn't even in dry-dock

yet. When Calvin Junior succumbs, Calvin
Senior is disconsolate, stroking his namesake's
forehead and sobbing in public. As one reporter
will put it, "He wept unafraid, unashamed."

He is like a shirt turned inside out—
all of the stitching is now apparent.
He'll wear a black armband for months,
heraldic emblem of an effusive woe.

He'll renounce presidential pomp,
experiencing what psychologists call
a dysphoric mood or major depressive
episode. The Resolute Desk, like the ship

from which it came, stuck in Arctic ice:
congressmen and cabinet members
waddling like penguins around him.
Call it fatherly love winning out in loss,

a touching, if somewhat dire, paralysis—
not the failure that historians like
to speak of, not a dereliction of duty.
No, the scrupulous fulfillment of another,

more basic one. Governor of Grief!
Chief Executive of Sorrow! Few politicians
have the talent to move a bill through
committee in the underworld.

I honor you Abe Lincoln, yet I've had
enough of your nobility, prosecuting a war
despite your own depression
and the loss of Willie. Your will

appalls me. Get on your mule and ride
out of Washington. I want a man
who *falls* to the occasion, who plummets
completely; a man whom reason

abandons. You can't have power *and*
a son—you can't even have one of them
for long, Calvin Senior will conclude.
I'm partial to such thinking

and to the sport that underlies it.
His very chair is perched on Roosevelt's
old baseline. How the Hero of San Juan Hill
loved to peg the members of his tennis

cabinet! His volley like a Gatling gun.
Spiro Agnew, the future's seedy kickback—
yes, time, the great developer, must pay
to play with lives—will bean his own

doubles partner, prompting Tricky Dick
to joke, "He ought to conduct diplomacy
in Cambodia with a racket!"
There's always darkness in a leader's strokes.

The past is like some terrible pollutant—
it gets into the groundwater;
the present is like an East European forest
where the animals have two heads

and the vegetables are radioactive.
For half a millennium, Richard III secretly
ruled England from beneath a London
carpark—think of him as directing traffic.

Whenever Calvin Senior looks out the window,
Calvin Junior is still hitting backhands.
He moves with the grace of a ghost,
unfettered by limbs or gravity.

BELIEF

1. The Man in the Water

It never seems more than a few days before the contention, the bickering, the tugging at the idol begins.—*Washington Post* editorial

Amidst the haze of falling snow and failing light, only the tail of the 737 is visible above the waterline.

An elderly gentleman, a bank examiner, helps a woman to tie a rope around her waist. He then

courteously passes it, once the helicopter has returned, to a fellow survivor. This passenger, the pilot

will later report, "seemed the most alert." After three of the five have been rescued (half-lifted

from, half-pulled across the shattered ice), the man points to another woman who has swum away from

the bobbing tail. Like a mother seal protecting its infant cub, the helicopter follows and pulls

her to safety as well. When, at last, it is his turn to be extricated, the bank examiner has disappeared

into the river's vault, into one of its many safe deposit boxes. (In winter, under Reagan, the Potomac doubles as a morgue—it lacks liquidity.) The helicopter pilot and paramedic search repeatedly

for the man. "We looked in the water," the latter will say, "in the wreck, everywhere, but he was gone....

The people who were saved owe their lives to him." The debt might as well be written on

their lungs—breath itself is a predatory loan.

                            To skip the snow fantastic—
that's what the passengers

of Air Florida Flight 90 wanted. A little sun, a little surf.... Because takeoff so quickly morphed

into landing, because the sky so quickly became a bridge and then a body of water, they

did not receive their formal summoning—the way the hero does in *Everyman*, that quaint, 15th-century

morality play. Or the way I did once on final approach to Warsaw when the jet shook violently

in a thunderstorm. The flight attendant said, "Make sure your seat-backs and tray-tables are in

their fully *uptight* and locked position. You'll be *in* the ground shortly." Unprepared for death,

the survivors were unprepared for wild generosity. The bank examiner wasn't counting assets, wasn't determining risk. No, he had renounced what that German duo called "the icy waters of egotistical calculation."

He was "the best we can do," as one journalist will describe him. All of Washington was submerged,

and *he* was rescuing us from our own insolvency. Days pass. I cling to the story, as to an inflatable raft

or to the very cross of Christ—until, that is, the divers go to work and they can't find anyone with

water in their lungs. Surely but surely, the dead are raised—I drive down to watch. The paper keeps

track of the salvage operation: "Recovered Wednesday," "Recovered Thursday," "Recovered Friday."

I can almost see Lazarus unwrapping that pun. The light is a haughty pathologist who takes pride in

her accomplishments. The first fifty perished from blunt force trauma. Like a politician switching parties

to win an election, the city turns on the phantom do-gooder. Our Johnny-on-the-spot is now an

illusion akin to what the dying see at the end of life. "Yet, what about the pilot and paramedic?" someone asks.

Well, they were mistaken. Even if the "Man in the Water" did exist, he was too hypothermic to think clearly, too dazed to be given credit for what he did. The skeptics are like sloth bears who eat their

young not twenty minutes after birthing them. Eventually, a suitable candidate emerges from the murk,

but he has a beard. The "Man in the Water" did not have a beard. Then others are lifted, from the Potomac,

and the experts alight on a bank examiner from Atlanta. How odd to look to the drowned for hope.

2. The Convict-Priest

He has a history of showing up at disaster scenes. He gains the confidence of the relatives and later burglarizes their houses.
—Police officer quoted in the *Washington Post*

Upon hearing of the crash, having already decamped from a prison in Danbury, CT, he drives down

to D.C. and rents a cassock and collar. I say "rents," but what I really mean is "pilfers" them from

a struggling costume store. (The car, too, is pinched.) Posing as a man of faith, a professional,

someone well-versed in the predicament of the drowned, he will set up shop at a hotel where the relatives

of the un-aired have gathered. The lobby has become a small chapel—no, more like a derangement park or carnival. The check-in lady sells tickets while the bellhops push mourners around on luggage

carts. Wailing goes wide in the end zone and drops a pass over and over— football is on replay.

The coffee remakes itself; it's as fresh as formaldehyde and smells nearly as clean. The carpet begs to be

dissected.
When the convict-cum-reverend arrives, Mary and Martha demand to know why he didn't appear

earlier. It's been two days since a giant loon took a nap on the floor of the Potomac; their brother is

inside. They need the reverend to wake it. To them, his arms—and cross— look like cranes. "The soul

is a simple balloon," he says. "A child walks on the beach and mistakenly releases it. Do not grieve;

watch it soar into the atmosphere. Its string is the scribbling hand of God." His words are like little

white pills or a fresh coat of paint in hell—he is the Willy Loman of the limbic system, the Martha Stewart

of less-than-optimal interiors. The man is fake, but his words are not, or, rather, his words are fake,

but their effect is not. Martha and Mary and Joan and Jill are moved. The reverend has his own runway now, and he gathers speed. It is like being at a Blue Angels show: the *Double Farvel*, the *Vixen*

Break, the *Section High-Alpha Pass*. What he can do with grief! Picture taffy in the sky, reason bending

into faith. The man could sell P.T. Barnum the afterlife! The reverend ushers mourners out into

the hotel parking lot. "Behold the river," he says. "Sometimes the saddest dead are like geese. Flapping and

flapping, they struggle to rise, but they do—eventually. Can you see them?" he asks. "There's one over

there. Her wings are still wet." Below, of course, the passengers remain in their seats, as obedient as

ever—the loon hasn't yet taxied to the gate. ("A little longer, folks. There's some congestion on the river

bottom.") That evening, the reverend appears on television: *Nightline with Ted Koppel*. He has the slick,

metallic skin of an airborne eel. His warden recognizes him, sends out an APB, at which point

he is apprehended—like a dog in a neighboring town or a prayer spoken aloud. The former is put back in

its pen; the latter, its mouth. The point of this parable? If it flies, it's false. (The framers, after all, owned slaves; the husband or wife commits adultery….) And yet, when asked about the eloquent impostor, Joan will

say, brought low by material fact yet nevertheless insistent, "The guy really helped me. He did."

NOTES

PAPER MAN
In 2016, a formerly unpublished interview with Ehrlichman revealed that America's "War on Drugs" was designed to help Nixon win election. From the interview: "The Nixon campaign in 1968, and the Nixon White House after that, had two enemies: the antiwar left and black people. ... We knew we couldn't make it illegal to be either against the war or blacks, but by getting the public to associate the hippies with marijuana and blacks with heroin. And then criminalizing both heavily, we could disrupt those communities. ...Did we know we were lying about the drugs? Of course we did." The term "bad bundle" refers to low quality heroin. A "paper boy" is someone who uses or sells heroin. To "chase the tiger" is to smoke heroin. A "jolly pop" is a new user. "Courage pills," "reindeer dust," and "white china" are all street names for heroin. The "Iron Chancellor" was H.R. Haldeman's nickname in the White House.

THE JUSTICE AND MY FATHER
At the beginning of each session of the Supreme Court, the marshal proclaims, "God save the United States and this honorable court."

THE USES OF CATASTROPHE
The woman who floundered in the icy water turned out to be a passenger, not a flight attendant. During the televised rescue, a friend of the flight attendant called in and insisted that the floundering woman was her friend. "We Move Our Tail for You" comes from an actual airline advertisement. In the *Iliad*, the river god Scamander speaks the lines that are quoted in the poem. *A Hero of Our Time* is a 19th-century Russian novel by Mikhail Lermontov.

LESSONS

The painter Winslow Homer moved to Prouts Neck, Maine in 1883 and produced his famous sea-scenes there in the mid-1880s. Caffarelli was the stage name for the 18th-century Italian castrato and opera singer Gaetano Majorano.

"THE LADY CRAZIES"

The concept of hysteria dates back to Ancient Greece when people believed that a woman's womb or uterus might wander throughout the body. According to one writer, "Doctors prescribed all kinds of different remedies to lure the uterus back to its seat. Women were told to rub honey on their vagina and chew cloves of garlic." The honey would attract; the garlic, repel. In the Middle Ages, a convent of "hysterical" French nuns meowed so regularly and continuously that a troop of soldiers threatened to make them stop. Another theory of hysteria concerned the "retention of female semen, which was thought to be stored in the uterus and to mingle with male semen during sex." Such semen would become venomous if a woman was not exposed to regular intercourse.

LITTLE FALLS

Hurricane Agnes killed 119 people in the United States and caused massive flooding. Agnes of Rome (c. 291-c. 304) was a virgin martyr. After refusing the advances of many a nobleman, she was labeled a Christian and dragged naked to a brothel. According to legend, her faith in Jesus caused her hair to grow, thereby concealing her body, and anyone who tried to rape her went blind. Eventually, she was beheaded. My Lai and Haditha are infamous American military massacres. Little Falls Dam was built in 1959 to provide water for Washington, D.C. Newspapers have referred to it as a "drowning machine."

THE COLUMNIST

William Safire was a columnist for the *New York Times* and the *New York Times Magazine*. "On Language" appeared regularly in the latter. *Before the Fall* is a memoir of Safire's time working as a speech writer for Nixon. Safire was a strong proponent of the Iraq War.

RIVER PORN

Chief of Staff under Nixon and Ford and Secretary of State under Reagan, General Haig famously declared, "I am in control here" after Reagan was shot. He was endlessly lampooned for ignoring the official line of succession. A rabid anti-communist, Haig played a key role in Reagan's decision to support the Contras.

AS FRANK CARLUCCI LAY DYING

Frank Carlucci served as both National Security Advisor and Secretary of Defense under Reagan. Patrice Lumumba was the first Prime Minister of the independent Democratic Republic of the Congo, a former Belgian colony. He was overthrown in a coup and executed after only a few months in power. Lumumba had sought the help of the US and UN in suppressing the Katangan secessionists. When they refused, he turned to the Soviet Union, setting off a crisis that led to his death.

DRAIN ENTRAPMENT INCIDENT

The Virginia Graeme Baker Pool and Spa Safety Act, which required all drains to be retrofitted, took effect in December of 2008. Roughly 3500 Iraqi civilians died during the Allies' Gulf War air campaign. The ground assault began with anti-mine plows, which had been mounted on tanks and armored earthmovers. These vehicles buried alive the Iraqi soldiers who were defending Saddam Hussein's desert trench network.

MEMORIAL DAY, 1990

Twenty-three U.S. servicemen were killed during the invasion of Panama in 1989. Its goal was to depose the country's leader, General Manuel

Noriega, who for years had been a paid CIA asset. To pressure him to step down, he was previously indicted on drug-related charges.

JANUARY SOJOURN
In 2006, during the Iraq War, five members of the 101st Airborne Division raped and murdered Abeer Qassim Hamza al-Janabi. They also killed her sister and parents.

PATTI DAVIS IS MY HERO
The Long Goodbye: Memories of My Fathers is the title of Davis's 2004 memoir. As President of the Screen Actors Guild, Reagan provided the FBI with the names of actors he thought were communist sympathizers. More than 20,000 Americans had died of AIDs before Reagan, in the sixth year of his presidency, gave a speech on the subject.

THE SLEEPING SENTINEL
Brigadier General William F. "Baldy" Smith gave the order for Private William Scott to be executed. Although Lincoln pardoned him, Smith insisted on teaching his troops a lesson by only revealing the pardon as Scott faced a firing squad. Scott's father, a Vermont farmer, traveled to Washington to thank the President who gave him ten dollars (roughly $280 dollars, adjusted for inflation) so that he could hire workers for his farm—all four of his sons were away fighting for the Union. Private Scott would die eight months later at the Battle of Lee's Mills. Two of his brothers would also die in combat; a third brother would die shortly after returning from the war. Mary Lincoln was institutionalized by her son Robert Todd in Batavia, Illinois, in 1875. By this point she had lost a third son. The italicized lines in section one are from a letter by Private Scott.

WHEN I WAS A TENNIS PRO
Actress and talk-show host Ellen DeGeneres was roundly criticized by the American Left for socializing with the 43rd president, George Walker

Bush, at a professional football game. The 41st president, George Herbert Walker Bush, served in the United States Navy in World War II. He flew a torpedo bomber, which was shot down in the Pacific theatre. Bush was the only crew member to survive.

GO TO HELL, ROBERT MUELLER
I am indebted to Rob Sears for turning the utterances of Donald Trump into poetry. I use part of "My hands are normal hands" in my poem. I also borrow lines from Anna Akhmatova's poem "Wild Honey."

THE MAN WHO CARED ABOUT HIS TEETH
Gogol is the author of a short story called "The Nose." In search of a more prominent job, a man's nose up and leaves his face. It is then seen all over St. Petersburg, dressed in the uniform of a high-ranking civil servant. The story satirizes the all-consuming interest in social rank. Gogol never finished his novel *Dead Souls*.

O CALVIN, O CALVIN
Born in Vermont, Calvin Coolidge was visiting his family home in Plymouth Notch when he received news that President Harding had died. Notoriously tight-lipped, Coolidge was so reluctant to speak in social situations that he once responded to a dinner guest, who had bet that he could get more than two words out of the Vice President, by saying, "You lose." After the death of his son Calvin Jr., the President claimed to have seen him playing on the White House court. Richard III was King of England from 1483-1485. He died at the Battle of Bosworth Field. His body was found in 2012 beneath a car park on the old site of the Greyfriars Church.

BELIEF
Arnold Dean Williams of Atlanta was determined to be the passenger who helped the other survivors—the passenger whom *Time* magazine dubbed "The Man in the Water." The 14th Street Bridge, which Air

Florida Flight 90 hit before plunging into the Potomac, was renamed in his honor.

ABOUT RALPH JAMES SAVARESE

Ralph James Savarese is the author of two books of prose, *Reasonable People* and *See It Feelingly*, and the co-editor of three collections. His creative work has appeared in *American Poetry Review, Fourth Genre, Modern Poetry In Translation, New England Review, Nine Mile Magazine, Ploughshares, Seneca Review, Sewanee Review,* and *Southwest Review*. He teaches at Grinnell College in Iowa.